USBORNE BEGINNERS

TRASH AND RECYCLING

Stephanie Turnbull

Designed by Andrea Slane and Michelle Lawrence

Illustrated by Christyan Fox

Trash and recycling consultant: Cecilia Davey, The Young People's
Trust for the Environment and Nature Conservation

Reading consultant: Alison Kelly,
Roehampton University

Contents

In the bin

Every day people throw away things that are empty, broken, used or just not wanted any more.

The amount of trash that is thrown away grows and grows.

Each person throws away about seven times their weight in trash every year.

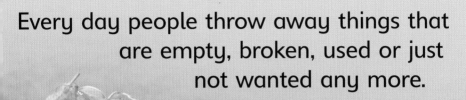

A load of garbage

Trash comes from many places.

People in houses, schools and offices throw lots of things away.

Factories, farms and building sites make trash too.

There is even trash floating in space. It is mostly pieces of old rockets.

Most trash is thrown into trash cans, but sometimes it is dropped on the ground or dumped in rivers and seas.

Dumped trash can spread disease and cut or poison wild animals.

Collection time

Trucks come to take away trash that has been left out in trash cans and bags.

This truck has a special lift that picks up big cans and empties them into the truck.

Panel inside the truck

Shovel

1. A shovel scoops trash in and packs it against a panel.

2. As the truck fills, the panel slides back to make more room.

3. More trash is added and is squashed up inside the truck.

The city of Venice, in Italy, has canals instead of streets so its trash is collected in boats.

On the move

When trash has been collected, it is taken to a place called a transfer station.

Trucks dump their loads of trash down a deep chute at the transfer station.

A heavy metal ram pushes the trash into enormous metal boxes.

Long, flat trucks carry the boxes to places where the trash will be buried or burned.

At some transfer stations, boxes are loaded onto ships or trains instead of trucks.

Some trains can carry more than 200 boxes of trash.

Buried deep

The boxes of trash are emptied out at a place called a landfill.

The trash is spread out and squashed by a compactor truck.

1. The compactor's wide, spiked wheels flatten the trash.

2. Diggers spread soil over the top of the trash.

3. The next day, new boxes of trash are added to the landfill.

4. The landfill grows bit by bit until it looks like a hill.

Full landfills are covered with grass. Soon there won't be enough land left to build new ones.

Up in flames

Some trash doesn't go to landfills.
Instead it is burned in an incinerator.

1. Trucks dump trash into a deep pit at the incinerator.

2. A grabber picks up the trash and feeds it into a huge fire.

3. Ash from the fire is put in a truck and taken to a landfill.

4. Smoke from the fire goes out of a tall chimney.

Hot air from incinerators can be used to heat homes and swimming pools.

This worker at an incinerator is checking the fire where trash is burned. His face is covered to protect it from the heat.

Dangerous waste

Some trash, such as chemicals and engine oil, can harm people, animals and the land.

This man is carrying a tub that contains dangerous chemicals.

The tub is sealed tightly and will be buried in a special landfill.

This is a landfill where chemicals have been buried. They are covered with a special white powder that seals them underground.

Some chemicals are burned in incinerators instead of being buried.

Spilled oil can poison water, so it must be cleaned up quickly.

Down the drain

Every time you take a bath or flush the toilet, the waste water flows away down underground pipes called sewers.

This photograph shows a robot about the size of a basketball. It moves through sewers to check for leaks inside the pipes.

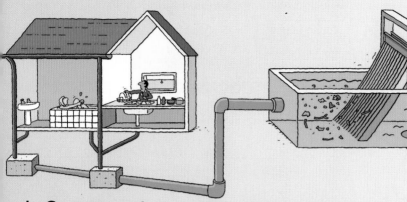

1. Sewers take waste, also called sewage, to a sewage works.

2. A screen traps big pieces of trash like rags and sticks.

3. The sewage goes into tanks where solid waste sinks.

4. The water is cleaned in other tanks then flows into lakes.

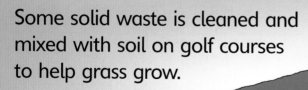

Some solid waste is cleaned and mixed with soil on golf courses to help grass grow.

Recycling

Some trash can be made into new things and used again. This is called recycling.

Paper, cardboard, glass, metal and plastic can all be recycled.

In some places there are collection trucks that pick up trash that can be recycled.

In other places, people take their cans, bottles and paper to big recycling bins.

The collected trash is sorted in factories. These men are checking cans and taking out anything that isn't metal.

There is often a symbol like this on things that can be recycled.

Melting metal

All kinds of metal can be melted down and used again. These pictures show how aluminum drink cans are recycled.

1. Cans are crushed into blocks, then a machine shreds them.

2. Hot air burns any patterns or logos off the pieces of metal.

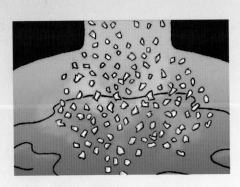

3. Next, the pieces of metal are heated until they melt.

4. The melted metal is poured into molds and left to cool.

Some metal cans are recycled into car or plane parts.

The metal hardens into blocks like these. Each block can be made into more than one million new cans.

21

Crushed glass

Used glass bottles and jars can be recycled again and again.

1. Old glass is dumped onto a moving belt at a recycling center.

2. Workers sort the glass and take out big pieces of trash.

3. Heavy rollers crush the glass into small pieces.

4. A vacuum sucks up any pieces of metal or scraps of paper.

Crushed glass is melted and shaped into new containers, ready to be filled again.

Old glass bottles can be crushed and mixed with gravel to make roads.

Piles of paper

When paper is recycled, it is mixed with water until it is a soggy mush. The mush then goes through different stages.

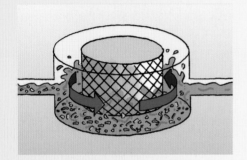

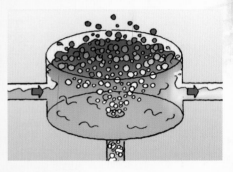

1. It is spun around. Staples and other parts fall to the bottom.

2. Next, soap cleans the mush and gets rid of ink and glue.

3. The mush is then sprayed out onto a moving wire screen.

4. It is squeezed by rollers, dried and wound into a big roll.

Recycled paper is made into all sorts of things. Here it has been turned into bedding for cows.

Paper can be recycled several times. Each time it could become a different product.

One big roll of recycled paper can make 80,000 rolls of toilet paper.

Fantastic plastic

Used plastic bottles can be recycled into soft, fleecy material for making clothes. These pictures show how it is done.

1. First, old plastic bottles are collected and sorted by color.

2. Next, the bottles are cleaned with strong jets of water.

3. Then the bottles are torn into pieces by metal rollers.

4. The pieces of plastic are melted into a sticky mess.

5. Melted plastic is pushed through holes to make long strands.

6. When the strands cool, they are woven into thick material.

This material is often used to make warm fleeces, like the one this climber is wearing.

Plastic bottles that aren't recycled take 800 years to rot away in a landfill.

27

Rotting away

Some trash, such as leaves and vegetable peelings, can be recycled into dark, thick soil called compost.

This machine chops up natural waste from people's yards and gardens. The waste will rot and turn into compost.

Some people have composting bins for all their fruit and vegetable waste.

The waste rots inside the bin. After a few weeks, it has turned into compost.

The compost can then be taken out and put on plants to help them grow.

Worms can be put in composting bins to eat waste and help to turn it into compost.

Glossary

Here are some of the words in this book you might not know. This page tells you what they mean.

 transfer station - a place where trucks take trash to be packed into boxes.

 landfill - an area of land that is filled with trash and covered with soil.

 compactor - a machine that spreads and flattens trash at a landfill.

 incinerator - a building where trash is taken to be burned.

 sewage works - a place where waste water is taken to be cleaned.

 aluminum - a silvery metal that is often used to make drink cans.

 compost - a crumbly soil made from rotted fruit, vegetables and other waste.

Websites to visit

If you have a computer, you can find out more about trash and recycling on the Internet. On the Usborne Quicklinks website there are links to four fun websites.

Website 1 - Sort trash for recycling in a fast-moving game.

Website 2 - Color a trash truck picture.

Website 3 - Find out how worms can help to recycle natural waste.

Website 4 - Play games to test how much you know about recycling.

To visit these websites, go to **www.usborne-quicklinks.com** and type the keywords "beginners trash". Then click on the link for the website you want to visit. Before you use the Internet, look at the safety guidelines inside the back cover of this book and ask an adult to read them with you.

Index

Acknowledgements

Photographic manipulation by Nick Wakeford, John Russell and Mike Wheatley

Americanization by Carrie Armstrong

Photo credits

The publishers are grateful to the following for permission to reproduce material:

© Alamy (Justin Case) 9, (Jeff Morgan) 19, 31, (John Foxx) 27; © John B. Boykin/CORBIS 1; © Robert Brook/ SCIENCE PHOTO LIBRARY 15; © Creatas 2-3; © Nature Picture Library (Michael Durham) 5; © Phil Matt/AGSTOCK/SCIENCE PHOTO LIBRARY 25; © Peter Menzel/SCIENCE PHOTO LIBRARY 16; © Novelis Recycling 21; © Rockware Glass 23; ©TEK IMAGE/SCIENCE PHOTO LIBRARY 14; © Keith Wood/CORBIS 13; © Viridor Waste Management 28-29; © zefa/Claudius 10